1001 WAYS TO
ENLIGHTENMENT

With special thanks to Anne Moreland

ARCTURUS

This edition published in 2013 by Arcturus Publishing Limited
26/27 Bickels Yard, 151–153 Bermondsey Street,
London SE1 3HA

ISBN: 978-1-84858-551-5
AD002247EN

Printed in China

Contents

Introduction

We all seek enlightenment of one kind or another. Perhaps our aim is to free ourselves from negative emotions like jealousy and low self-esteem, that lead us to behave in ways we don't like; and that may, we feel, limit our true potential. Alternatively, we may be seeking a deeper meaning and purpose for our lives, asking ourselves the big questions: why we're born, why we die, and how best we can live out our short but precious life span in between? Some of us might want more knowledge still: to experience, through self-discipline and meditative practice, the heightened states of awareness attained by some of the great religious and spiritual leaders of the past, as well as the guides of the present.

Whatever our quest, learning from the experiences of others, whether famous spiritual teachers or wise individuals, must be our first step on the path to enlightenment. This little book, packed full of wisdom and advice, can't guarantee to help you reach your goal, for, as you will find out, each person must find his or her own way; but it promises to be a good companion, a faithful fellow-traveller, as you set out on your journey.

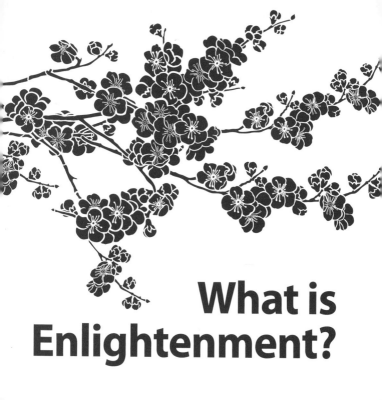

What is
Enlightenment?

What do we mean by 'enlightenment'? Is it simply a process of shedding light on a subject or problem, through rational thought, or is it more mysterious than that – a kind of spiritual awakening? Or even, perhaps, an understanding of what our true purpose in life consists of, and how we can best spend our days?

None of us set out on the path of enlightenment without first resolving to improve our lives.

To be free from suffering, desire, and negative emotions: that is enlightenment.

If we always try to move forward in life, learning from our experiences rather than being limited by them, we move towards enlightenment.

A wonderful film, book, or play can enlighten us: it can make us understand our world, our selves and our fellow human beings better than we did before.

Listen, rather than speak; observe, rather than rush by; be sensitive, rather than ego-driven.

Finding enlightenment is like seeing the light at the end of the tunnel, and knowing that one day, you will emerge into it.

**Anger and intolerance
are the enemies of
correct understanding.**
Mahatma Gandhi

**True enlightenment
doesn't have to be a
religious experience,
but it is always a
spiritual one.**

To feel peaceful, contented, happy, and at one with the world is not always easy; at best, it may be a fleeting emotion.

For most of us, enlightenment does not come suddenly, but little by little, as we begin to understand more about ourselves and the world around us.

Travel is fatal to prejudice, bigotry, and narrow-mindedness... Broad, wholesome, charitable views of men and things cannot be acquired by vegetating in one little corner of the earth all one's lifetime.

Mark Twain

Life is a beautiful gift, if we only know how to receive it.

If you want to jump high over an obstacle, you must take a long run up to it first.

When we are well, we often overlook the fact that health is a great blessing; it is only when we become sick that we realize how lucky we once were.

How far you go in life depends on your being tender with the young, compassionate with the aged, sympathetic with the striving, and tolerant of the weak and strong. Because some day in life you will have been all of these.

George Washington Carver

Leave the past behind; relish the present; and trust in the future.

When you lose, don't lose heart.

Discovery is the ability to be puzzled by simple things.

Noam Chomsky

Enlightenment is freedom: freedom from pain, suffering, and ignorance.

Don't seek to define enlightenment; it is indefinable, yet you will know it when it arrives.

A table, a chair, a bowl of fruit, and a violin: what else does man need to be happy?

Albert Einstein

There is nothing
to stop you from
understanding
who you are
and what you
might become.

**The enlightened person is wise,
kind, tolerant, and above all,
receptive to others.**

Self-doubt is part of the process of self-discovery.

Not everything that is faced can be changed. But nothing can be changed until it is faced.

James Baldwin

Courage and confidence is gained from every challenge that you meet and overcome in life.

No one, when he has lit a lamp, puts it in a cellar or under a basket, but on a stand, that those who come in may see the light.
The Bible

Enlightened minds are educated minds – but the education may be that of life, rather than that of learning.

In the practice of tolerance, one's enemy is the best teacher. *Tenzin Gyatso*

To find enlightenment, you need to have faith in yourself, and in your ability to reach your destiny.

Each morning, when the sun comes up, you have another chance to find enlightenment, both literal and metaphorical.

To live with love and generosity is to live well.

The truth is sometimes spoken in words, and sometimes in silence.

Gaining self-respect is the first step on the path to enlightenment.

I do not want the peace that passeth understanding. I want the understanding that bringeth peace.

Helen Keller

A bulb under the earth grows towards the light, in order to flower; in the same way, we move instinctively towards enlightenment.

Trying to reach a deeper understanding of others is one way of reaching a deeper understanding of oneself.

Moderation in all things.

A morning-glory at my window satisfies me more than the metaphysics of books.
Walt Whitman

Great oaks from little acorns grow.

An enlightened society, in which all are treated and valued equally, is the true goal of humanity.

Live your life daily in a way that you never lose yourself. When you are carried away with your worries, fears, cravings, anger, and desire, you run away from yourself and you lose yourself. The practice is always to go back to oneself.

Thich Nhat Hanh

Life is too short for regrets. Learn lessons from your mistakes, and go forward.

In the game of life, we can decide on the rules, and the stakes, but not on when to quit.

Reason is one of our greatest gifts; we must use it.

To forgive is indeed the best form of self-interest since anger, resentment, and revenge are corrosive of that 'summum bonum', the greatest good.

Desmond Tutu

Enlightenment is the harvest time of the mind.

In life, we either follow paths or make our own trails.

Your vision will become clear only when you can look into your own heart.

Carl Jung

Lightening the load; lightening the dark: enlightenment.

Where do we find enlightenment? In a learned book; in a spiritual ritual; in contemplation; looking at a beautiful painting; or simply in the joy of being alive?

**When in doubt, say nothing.
Other people will fill the silence.**

To be nobody but yourself in a world which
is doing its best, night and day, to make you
everybody else, means to fight the hardest
battle which any human being can fight;
and never stop fighting. *E.E. Cummings*

The most dangerous lies are the ones you tell yourself.

Enlightenment comes at the beginning of the road, when we first learn that we must travel; and at the end, when we look back at where we have come from.

Making your mark on the world is hard. If it were easy, everybody would do it. But it's not. It takes patience, it takes commitment, and it comes with plenty of failure along the way. The real test is not whether you avoid this failure, because you won't. It's whether you let it harden and shame you into inaction, or whether you learn from it; whether you choose to persevere. *Barack Obama*

The enlightened minds of the past speak to us from down the centuries, in the records of their thinking that they left behind.

When I dare to be powerful, to use my strength in the service of my vision, then it becomes less and less important whether I am afraid.

Audre Lorde

We never stop making mistakes; and we must never stop learning from them.

The enlightened teacher does not show the way, but simply describes the path he or she once took.

Governing anger, and controlling the ego, are both crucial to becoming enlightened.

Always read between the lines.

When people talk, listen completely. Most people never listen.

Ernest Hemingway

Unlock the door to your mind, and to the great mystery contained therein.

You are the creator of every experience you have.

Enlightenment must come little by little – otherwise it would overwhelm.

Idries Shah

The seeker after the truth always remains a seeker; for complete enlightenment can never be found.

Peace; love; compassion; wisdom; kindness: a way of life.

Enlightenment is not imagining figures of light but making the darkness conscious.
Carl Jung

The sleeping secret of enlightenment lies within you, if only you can awaken it.

Everyone is truly an enlightened being, if only in potential.

It is the mark of an educated mind to be able to entertain a thought without accepting it.
Aristotle

Enlightenment is a tranquil state of self beyond the clamour of the ego.

Everyone has experienced enlightenment at some time or another: that sudden shift of consciousness, when you feel at one with the world around you, your place secure and peaceful.

Just as when you bite into an apple, you recognize the taste, when you touch enlightenment, you know what you are feeling.

Watch your thoughts; they become words.
Watch your words; they become actions.
Watch your actions; they become habits.
Watch your habits; they become character.
Watch your character; it becomes your destiny.

Lao Tzu

Consider the miracle of the flower, blossoming in beauty and grace, through a combination of reasons that we can never fully understand.

The question 'Who am I'? is the first we seek to answer when we set out on the road to enlightenment.

**There are only two ways to live your life.
One is as though nothing is a miracle.
The other is as if everything is.**

Albert Einstein

When you lose faith,
you lose the essence of life.

You cannot teach a man anything; you can only help him find it within himself.

Galileo

Don't be afraid of death; be afraid of failing to live to the full.

When you set out on the journey to enlightenment, you will have no map to tell you of your final destination.

Minds are like parachutes; they only function when they are open. *Thomas Dewar*

Make your morning salutation to the sun.
Stop for a moment as you go about your day,
and let the rays of its light warm you for a
moment or two.

Quiet words will win loud arguments.

Seeking enlightenment, through learning and experience, is the ultimate goal of both.

Don't ask, what's the answer; rather ask, what's the question.

Disappointment can only hurt you for as long as you let it; instead of looking back, try to move on, to the next challenge.

Tell me to what you pay attention and I will tell you who you are.

José Ortega y Gasset

Your real friends will tell you the truth; your false ones, only lies.

It's hard to accept failure, but sometimes even harder to live with success.

Real knowledge is to know the extent of one's ignorance.
Confucius

Where there's life, there's hope.

What we see depends mainly on what we look for. ***John Lubbock***

Hang a bird feeder outside your window; plant a sweet-smelling herb on your windowsill. Watching nature unfold and take its course will help you to think, and to feel peace.

You can only do your best in life, and no more.

Better to light a candle than curse the darkness.

Eleanor Roosevelt

The enlightened parent seeks to nurture; the authoritarian one, only to criticize and blame.

Every task in life requires practice; without repetition, we never learn.

The darkness of the soul is a fearful one; but after the longest night, comes the day, when the light of the sun dispels all shadows.

When you feel angry, upset, or at odds with yourself, ask the question: what is it I want? You may find you already have more than you realized.

Attitude is a little thing that makes a big difference.

Winston Churchill

A truly enlightened person is one who can understand the bad in people, as well as the good.

Your fate is not decided for you. You must create it, and follow it.

Some people dream of success; others work for it.

It is not enough to have a good mind; the main thing is to use it well.

René Descartes

Tears of sadness are the rivers of our mind, washing clean our souls, so that we can begin afresh, once our sorrow is over.

There is nothing permanent in life, except change.

We are not human beings having a spiritual experience, we are spiritual beings having a human experience.

Pierre Teilhard de Chardin

Enlightenment begins where ignorance and fear end.

Begin your new life today!
Treat people as if they
were what they ought to
be, and you'll help them
become what they are
capable of being.

**It is not enough to be busy.
So are the ants. The question is,
what are we busy about?**
Henry David Thoreau

The Path

There are many different paths to enlightenment; for example, through study, religion or spiritual disciplines. But the true way to enlightenment is the simplest, and perhaps also the hardest: through living life to the full, in all its richness and complexity, especially when times get tough.

Gaining spiritual enlightenment is a gradual process – step by step, one day at a time.

A teacher or leader can only tell you about the path he or she took, not about the one that you must take.

Be not angry that you cannot make others as you wish them to be, since you cannot make yourself as you wish yourself to be.

Thomas à Kempis

Nirvana is the state of being free from suffering, in which we 'blow out' the fires of hatred, greed, and delusion that threaten to consume our souls.

**Don't look where you fall,
but where you slipped.**

African proverb

Being loved by many people is not as
important as being loved by one person.

**Sitting by the fireside
warms the mind, as
well as the body.**

Enlightenment, or liberation of the mind, only comes through spiritual practice, which often takes a lifetime.

The five steps to enlightenment: Peace; Awareness; Intelligence; Freedom; Transcendence.

**Don't wait for the Last Judgement.
It happens every day.** *Albert Camus*

Enlightenment is a deep insight into the
meaning and purpose of all things.

Through craving, anger, and conflicting desire, human beings cause themselves much suffering. Enlightenment is freedom from such destructive emotions, but it does not come without a cost; it must be fought for, and worked for, over many years.

Growing up is something you choose to do, not something you have to do.

What saves a man is to take a step; then another step; then another. It is always the same step, but you have to take it.

Antoine de Saint-Exupéry

The enlightened soul is fully awake to reality, in all its beauty and complexity, yet untouched by it.

The eightfold path of the Buddha:
Right view
Right aspiration
Right speech
Right action
Right livelihood
Right effort
Right mindfulness
Right concentration

The enlightened mind sees the unity of every phenomenon on the planet, including its own place within it.

We are more treacherous through weakness than through calculation.

François de La Rochefoucauld

Enlightenment is a change of consciousness in which one's own personal desires are seen in context, as part of a whole, and therefore not overwhelmingly important.

Don't judge each day by the harvest you reap, but by the seeds that you plant.

Robert Louis Stevenson

Seekers after truth must learn, first and foremost, how to free themselves from their own selfish desires and needs.

Some scientists believe that during meditation, when the subject experiences enlightenment, the brain actually shows measurable changes in activity.

See everything; overlook a great deal; correct a little.
Pope John XXIII

Nirvana: awakening; understanding; freedom from suffering, desire, and ignorance.

Enlightenment comes when the ego is banished from the mind, and replaced by compassion, wisdom, and skill.

Anyone can carry his burden, however hard, until nightfall. Anyone can do his work, however hard, for one day. Anyone can live sweetly, patiently, lovingly, purely, till the sun goes down. And this is all life really means.

Robert Louis Stevenson

Enlightenment is a state of freedom from the ignorance that causes suffering.

Focussing on the present moment is a powerful way of banishing misery: for, without a sense of the future, we crave nothing, and without a sense of the past, we regret nothing.

Enjoy when you can, and endure when you must.

Johann Wolfgang von Goethe

Watching a spectacular sunset tells us nothing, except how good it is to be alive, and how small we are in comparison to the universe.

The price you paid to get what you used to want is what you have become.

Enlightenment may come through years of study, or in a single moment, witnessing the unfolding beauty of a flower.

If you surrender to the wind, you can ride it.

Toni Morrison

Rule the clock; do not be ruled by it.

Spending your life wishing for security is the best way to feel insecure.

Have courage for the great sorrows of life and patience for the small ones; and when you have laboriously accomplished your task, go to sleep in peace.
Victor Hugo

An ability to see the meaning and purpose of small events in life is a necessity if the mind is to become enlightened.

Unburden your mind, and you unburden your body.

**We have to live today by what truth
we can get today, and be ready
tomorrow to call it falsehood.**
William James

To love is to know; and to know is to love.

We are all gardeners, tending the seeds of days in the garden of eternity.

When you are ashamed of yourself, learn from what you have done, and then leave it behind you, as you would a load that has become too heavy to carry.

Seek freedom and become captive of your desires. Seek discipline and find your liberty.
Frank Herbert

Look before you leap; twice, if necessary.

Inspiration does not always come in a flash; it is more often the result of perspiration.

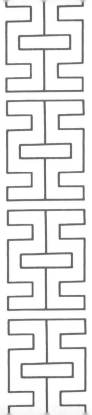

The first and greatest victory is to conquer yourself; to be conquered by yourself is of all things most shameful and vile.

Plato

Believe in yourself; accept what you are, and who you are. But don't be self-satisfied; that is not the same thing.

The active, watchful mind is one in which memory and thought bear on the moment, to produce 'presence of mind'.

Pick battles big enough to matter, small enough to win. *Jonathan Kozol*

Fear is the greatest obstacle on the path to enlightenment.

The practice of mindfulness can be achieved by focussing on the breath, faithfully returning to do so whenever the mind wanders.

Study; repeat; reflect; remember; remind.

Mindfulness:
of the heavens
of stopping and resting
of discipline
of breathing
of the body
of death

The vow that binds too strictly snaps itself.

Alfred Lord Tennyson

Enlightenment is not something we achieve, but something we may catch a glimpse of every day, until the time comes when we see the truth for more than just a moment.

A breathtaking sky; a beautiful flower; a deep, blue ocean; a field of corn; a sense that we are at one with nature. This is enlightenment.

What a strange narrowness of mind now is that, to think the things we have not known are better than the things we have known.

Samuel Johnson

To seek enlightenment is not to seek other-worldliness; it is to seek the here and now, in all its glory.

Life is a theatre; don't sleep through the show!

To see a world in a grain of sand
And heaven in a wild flower
Hold infinity in the palm of your hand
And eternity in an hour.

William Blake

Reflection brings us to enlightenment, where there is no need for reflection.

Everything that we see in the world teaches us something, even if it is only that we do not wish to see more.

Chaos and mystery are part of life, just as order and clarity are.

It is every man's obligation to put back into the world at least the equivalent of what he takes out of it.

Albert Einstein

Be swift to praise and slow to condemn.

To follow the light, one must be able to walk through darkness.

If only I may grow: firmer, simpler, quieter, warmer.
Dag Hammarskjöld

As a flower turns its head towards the sunlight, so our hearts, quite naturally, turn towards knowledge and understanding.

In order for you to know others, you must first know yourself.

Have a heart that never hardens, a temper that never tires, a touch that never hurts.

Charles Dickens

Anger and violence are
the enemies of love,
not only towards others,
but towards oneself.

**Make a footprint on
the sand of time;
don't sit and let it run
through your hands.**

Live life to the full, rather than spending it trying to avoid death, which must surely come one day.

In this age, which believes there is a short cut to everything, the greatest lesson to be learned is that the most difficult way is, in the long run, the easiest. *Henry Miller*

An enlightened person talks a little more quietly; walks a little slower; notices a little more, both about things and people; and listens carefully, whatever voices or sounds are heard.

Whatever you are, be a good one.
Abraham Lincoln

Love will be your faithful guide on the path to enlightenment.

Better to fight for a cause than against it.

Whether or not you choose to partake in life, it will continue just the same.

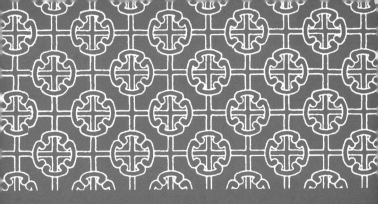

Create each day anew by clothing yourself with heaven and earth, bathing yourself with wisdom and love, and placing yourself in the heart of Mother Nature.

Morihei Ueshiba

In the day, take your time; in the night, take your rest.

It is impossible to stand still.
Standing still means going backwards,
since the world rushes on ahead.

Giving up doesn't always mean you have failed. Sometimes it is a sign that you are strong enough to let go.

The wind and the waves, the storm and the seas, the rain and the snow; these are not our friends, but neither are they our enemies.

Be still like a mountain and flow like a great river.
Lao Tzu

No matter how tall your grandfather was, you must do your own growing.
Irish proverb

Old age, to the unenlightened, is winter; to the enlightened, it is harvest time.

We must have passed through life unobservant, if we have never perceived that a man is very much himself what he thinks of others.

Frederick Faber

To reach the top of the mountain, you must first pass through the foothills.

Life is a question of paying attention to details; that is the way we pay attention to the larger issues.

Beware a man of one book.

English proverb

If you fail, don't forget the lessons that failure teaches you.

A small leak will sink a great ship.

Benjamin Disraeli

Passion is like the wind that fills the sails of a ship; if it blows too hard, the ship will sink; but if it doesn't blow at all, the ship cannot sail on.

We learn from listening to others; but we must also learn from listening to ourselves.

The best way to predict your future is to create it.

Peter Drucker

Your character is your destiny. Don't squander it.

Experience is the best, and sternest teacher.

There are times when reality must be confronted, however painful it may be to do so.

Never make your home in a place. Make a home for yourself inside your own head. You'll find what you need to furnish it – memory, friends you can trust, love of learning, and other such things. That way, it will go with you wherever you journey.

Tad Williams

Make the most of your life. You may have less time left than you think.

If you are quick to choose your friends, you may be quick to change them.

Kindness speaks softly; anger too loud.

The three great essentials to achieve anything worthwhile are, first, hard work; second, stick-to-itiveness; third, common sense. *Thomas Edison*

Aspire to treat everyone you meet with respect, courtesy, and kindness.

Even a clock that has stopped is right twice a day.

Before you cut, make sure you measure.

Tell me, and I'll forget. Show me, and I'll try to remember. Share with me, and I'll learn.

A man is rich in proportion to the number of things he can afford to let alone.

Henry David Thoreau

Dig the well before you become thirsty.

Chinese proverb

Life is not an event that is about to begin. It is not a test that you must prepare for. It is what is happening this minute ... so be ready, now.

In every fear there is a desire.
Sigmund Freud

Our emotions can function as a tight knot, binding us close and preventing us from breaking out and fulfilling our true potential as human beings.

Through dreaming, just as much as waking, we may find the path to enlightenment.

Your future depends on circumstance; and on you.

When you throw dirt, you lose ground.

The future lies before you
Like a path of pure, white snow.
Be careful how you tread in it
For every step will show.

To know the road ahead, ask those coming back.
Chinese proverb

The first principle is that you must not fool yourself, and you're the easiest person to fool. *Richard Feynman*

Being polite but firm will achieve more than being angry; for when you lose self-control, you show others that you have lost control over the situation, too.

There is an element of pure pleasure in enlightenment: in the satisfaction, however fleeting, of finally arriving in a place where one is at peace with oneself and the world.

God is good, but never dance in a small boat.

Irish proverb

It is better to raise a problem without solving it than to solve a problem without raising it.

To have a true evaluation of oneself is the most difficult thing in the world to achieve, but without it, we can never truly know what we are capable of.

The enlightened mind moves from darkness and sleep into life, awakening to the true nature of reality.

We are more often afraid of what we can do than what we can't.

Lust, malice, and delusion: these are the 'three fires' that rage through the dense forests of our minds, and that must be quenched before we can find peace.

You may find that you meet your destiny on the road you take to avoid it.

Find love; find peace; find happiness; find contentment; and, last, but not least, find enlightenment.

The Guides

Many spiritual teachers, both religious and secular, have guided their students on the path to enlightenment. There have also been great scientists, artists, entertainers and anonymous voices from history who have given us their thoughts on life.

People only see what they are prepared to see.

Ralph Waldo Emerson

Believe those who are seeking the truth. Doubt those who find it.

André Gide

Always keep your mind as bright and clear as the vast sky, the great ocean, and the highest peak, empty of all thoughts. Always keep your body filled with light and heat. Fill yourself with the power of wisdom and enlightenment.

Morihei Ueshiba

If I could define enlightenment briefly I would say it is 'the quiet acceptance of what is'.

Wayne Dyer

Losing an illusion makes you wiser than finding the truth.

Ludwig Börne

Those who really seek the path to enlightenment dictate terms to their minds. Then they proceed with strong determination. *Buddha*

Nirvana, or lasting enlightenment, or true spiritual growth, can be achieved only through persistent exercise of real love.
M. Scott Peck

Beware lest you lose the substance by grasping at the shadow. *Aesop*

If we remove ourselves from the world, we are pretending that we can follow our own individual enlightenment and let the rest of the world go to hell. **Satish Kumar**

Ignorance has always been the weapon of tyrants; enlightenment the salvation of the free.
Bill Richardson

From the enlightenment of music comes the wisdom of silence.

There is no enlightenment outside daily life.
Thich Nhat Hanh

**The obscure we see eventually.
The completely obvious, it
seems, takes longer.**
Edward R. Murrow

A wise man can see more from
the bottom of a well than a fool
can from a mountain top.

The real meaning of enlightenment is to gaze with undimmed eyes on all darkness. *Nikos Kazantzakis*

Unity is divinity, purity is enlightenment.

Sri Sathya Sai Baba

The map is not the territory.

Alfred Korzybski

The only Zen you can find on the tops of mountains is the Zen you bring up there.

Robert M. Pirsig

When you look into an abyss, the abyss also looks into you.

Friedrich Nietzsche

It is not the simple statement of facts that ushers in freedom; it is the constant repetition of them that has this liberating effect. Tolerance is the result not of enlightenment, but of boredom.

Quentin Crisp

Just being the seeker, somebody who is open to spiritual enlightenment, is in itself the important thing, and it's the reward for being a seeker in this world. *Walter Isaacson*

I am a part of all that I have met.

Alfred Lord Tennyson

Many spiritual teachers – in Buddhism, in Islam – have talked about first-hand experience of the world as an important part of the path to wisdom, to enlightenment.

Bell Hooks

We are all but recent leaves on the same old tree of life, and if this life has adapted itself to new functions and conditions, it uses the same old basic principles over and over again. There is no real difference between the grass and the man who mows it.

Albert Szent-Györgyi

The more we can understand and embrace enlightenment, the less need there is for chemical enhancement.
Kyan Douglas

Don't miss the doughnut by looking through the hole.

There is no fundamental difference between the preparation for death and the practice of dying, and spiritual practice leading to enlightenment. ***Stanislav Grof***

To learn something new, take the path that you took yesterday. *John Burroughs*

Enlightened people seldom or never possess a sense of responsibility.
George Orwell

Sometimes it's necessary to go a long distance out of the way in order to come back a short distance correctly. *Edward Albee*

Everybody wants to get enlightened but nobody wants to change.
Andrew Cohen

I know of no safe depository of the ultimate powers of the society but the people themselves; and if we think them not enlightened enough to exercise their control with a wholesome discretion, the remedy is not to take it from them but to inform their discretion.

Thomas Jefferson

He is a hypocrite who professes what he does not believe; not he who does not practice all he wishes or approves.

William Hazlitt

Not when truth is dirty, but when it is shallow, does the enlightened man dislike to wade into its waters.

Friedrich Nietzsche

The divine right of husbands, like the divine right of kings, may, it is hoped, in this enlightened age, be contested without danger.

Mary Wollstonecraft

Everyone has a spirit that can be refined, a body that can be trained in some manner, a suitable path to follow. You are here to realize your inner divinity and manifest your innate enlightenment.

Morihei Ueshiba

We are spirits clad in veils.

Christopher P. Cranch

The greatness of America lies not in being more enlightened than any other nation, but rather in her ability to repair her faults.
Alexis de Tocqueville

**The more enlightened our houses are,
the more their walls ooze ghosts.**
Italo Calvino

Before I travelled my road,
I was my road. *Antonio Porchia*

**To believe with
certainty we must
begin with doubting.**
King Stanisław I of Poland

The only people available to change the world are the people now living in it, with all the beliefs they bring along – however retrograde those beliefs may appear to those of us who see ourselves as enlightened. **Todd Gitlin**

The true grandeur of humanity is in moral elevation, sustained, enlightened and decorated by the intellect of man. *Charles Sumner*

All compromise is based on give and take, but there can be no compromise on fundamentals.

Mahatma Gandhi

The most successful people are those who are good at Plan B.

James Yorke

A hero is someone who understands the responsibility that comes with his freedom.
Bob Dylan

Contempt is the weapon of the weak, and a defense against one's own despised and unwanted feelings.
Alice Miller

This dragonfly came up to me. He was hovering right in front of my face, and I was really examining him, thinking, How does he see me? I became enlightened.

Ziggy Marley

Our greatest pretences are built up not to hide the evil and the ugly in us, but our emptiness. The hardest thing to hide is something that is not there. *Eric Hoffer*

Who is more foolish, the child afraid of the dark or the man afraid of the light?

Maurice Freehill

We stumble and fall constantly even when we are most enlightened. But when we are in true spiritual darkness, we do not even know that we have fallen. **Thomas Merton**

Seeking is not always the way to find.
Augustus Hare

It takes all the running you can do
just to keep in the same place.
Lewis Carroll

**You are today where your thoughts have
brought you; you will be tomorrow where
your thoughts take you.** *James Allen*

Though you may travel the world to find the beautiful, you must have it within you or you will find it not.
Ralph Waldo Emerson

When one tugs at a single thing in nature, he finds it hitched to the rest of the universe.

John Muir

Only in the early morning light of day, and of life, can we see the world without its shadows. Truth requires new beginnings.

Jeb Dickerson

One day, someone showed me a glass of water that was half full. And he said, 'Is it half full or half empty'? So I drank the water. No more problem.

Alejandro Jodorowsky

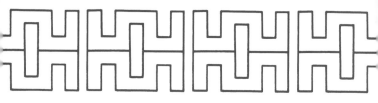

Borrowing knowledge of reality from all sources, taking the best from every study, Science of Mind brings together the highest enlightenment of the ages.

Ernest Holmes

A gun gives you the body, not the bird.
Henry David Thoreau

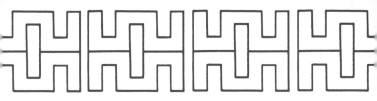

What you are aware of, you are in control of; what you are not aware of is in control of you.

Anthony de Mello

Happiness is when what you think, what you say, and what you do are in harmony.

Mahatma Gandhi

What deep wounds ever closed without a scar?
Lord Byron

Courage is not the absence of fear, but rather the judgement that something else is more important than fear.
Ambrose Redmoon

Sometimes the questions are complicated and the answers simple. *Dr Seuss*

You never know what is enough until you know what is more than enough.

William Blake

It is better to know some of the questions than all of the answers.
James Thurber

One does what one is; one becomes what one does. *Robert Musil*

Change is certain. Peace is followed by disturbances; departure of evil men by their return. Such recurrences should not constitute occasions for sadness but realities for awareness, so that one may be happy in the interim.

Percy Bysshe Shelley

A man who dares to waste one hour of time has not discovered the value of life.

Charles Darwin

It isn't until you come to a spiritual understanding of who you are – not necessarily a religious feeling, but deep down, the spirit within – that you can begin to take control.

Oprah Winfrey

Achievement of your happiness is the only moral purpose of your life, and that happiness, not pain or mindless self-indulgence, is the proof of your moral integrity, since it is the proof and the result of your loyalty to the achievement of your values. *Ayn Rand*

You have to expect things of yourself before you can do them. **Michael Jordan**

Life can only be understood backwards; but it must be lived forwards. *Søren Kierkegaard*

A man's work is nothing but this slow trek to rediscover, through the detours of art, those two or three great and simple images in whose presence his heart first opened.

Albert Camus

Art is always and everywhere the secret confession, and at the same time the immortal movement of its time.
Karl Marx

Truth can be found for ourselves, and in ourselves.

Old friends pass away, new friends appear. It is just like the days. An old day passes, a new day arrives. The important thing is to make it meaningful: a meaningful friend – or a meaningful day. *Dalai Lama*

Change will not come if we wait for some other person or some other time. We are the ones we've been waiting for. We are the change that we seek.

Barack Obama

The conscious mind may be compared to a fountain playing in the sun and falling back into the great subterranean pool of subconscious from which it rises.
Sigmund Freud

In the attitude of silence the soul finds the path in a clearer light, and what is elusive and deceptive resolves itself into crystal clearness. Our life is a long and arduous quest after Truth. *Mahatma Gandhi*

Those who wish to sing always find a song. *Swedish proverb*

Education is a way of living, not a preparation for life.

Let him that would move the world first move himself.

Robert Frost

Yesterday is but today's memory, and tomorrow is today's dream.
Khalil Gibran

Get the facts first. You can distort them later.
Mark Twain

We either make ourselves miserable, or we make ourselves strong.
The amount of work is the same.
Carlos Castaneda

The eternal mystery of the world is its comprehensibility.

Albert Einstein

The hardest victory is the victory over self. ***Aristotle***

Every man's life ends the same way. It is only the details of how he lived and how he died that distinguish one man from another.

Ernest Hemingway

Live without pretending, love without depending, listen without defending, speak without offending.

Drake

It's not where you came from that matters; it's where you're going.

I pay no attention whatever to anybody's praise or blame.
I simply follow my own feelings.
Wolfgang Amadeus Mozart

Float like a butterfly, sting like a bee.

Muhammad Ali

I can live alone, if self-respect, and circumstances require me so to do. I need not sell my soul to buy bliss. I have an inward treasure born with me, which can keep me alive if all extraneous delights should be withheld, or offered only at a price I cannot afford to give.

Charlotte Brontë

The wisest mind has something yet to learn.

George Santayana

To seek enlightenment is a choice that requires effort at times.

Action may not bring happiness, but there is no happiness without action.

Benjamin Disraeli

Inspiration and genius – one and the same.

Victor Hugo

The true test of character is not how much we know how to do, but how we behave when we don't know what to do.

John Holt

Character cannot be developed in ease and quiet. Only through experience of trial and suffering can the soul be strengthened, ambition inspired, and success achieved.

Helen Keller

Ageing is not lost youth but a new stage of opportunity and strength. *Betty Friedan*

Do not seek enlightenment; live as well as you can, and enlightenment will find you.

Weeping may endure for a night; but joy cometh in the morning.
The Bible

Deep experience is never peaceful.
Henry James

He does not believe who does not live according to his belief.

Thomas Fuller

Every road leads in two directions.
Russian proverb

Faith is a passionate intuition.
William Wordsworth

Darkness cannot drive out darkness; only light can do that. Hate cannot drive out hate; only love can do that.
Martin Luther King

Have faith and pursue the unknown end.

Oliver Wendell Holmes

Come forth into the light of things, let nature be your teacher.

William Wordsworth

Hope, like faith, is nothing if it is not courageous; it is nothing if it is not ridiculous.
Thornton Wilder

We shall draw from the heart of suffering itself the means of inspiration and survival.
Winston Churchill

Enlighten the people generally, and tyranny and oppressions of body and mind will vanish like evil spirits at the dawn of the day.

Thomas Jefferson

Because things are the way they are, things will not stay the way they are.

Bertolt Brecht

Kindness is a mark of faith, and whoever is not kind has no faith.
The Prophet Mohammed

Be alive to the light of the world, as well as the darkness.

Hope is the thing with feathers that perches in the soul – and sings the tunes without the words – and never stops at all. ***Emily Dickinson***

Love abounds in all things,
Excels from the depths to beyond the stars,
Is lovingly disposed to all things.
She has given the king on high
The kiss of peace. *Hildegard of Bingen*

Three things cannot long be hidden: the sun, the moon, and the truth. *Buddha*

Distance lends enchantment to the view. *Mark Twain*

The greatest wealth is health. *Virgil*

All changes, even the most longed for, have their melancholy; for what we leave behind us is a part of ourselves; we must die to one life before we can enter another.

Anatole France

Gardens are a form of autobiography.

Sydney Eddison

An eye for an eye only ends up making the whole world blind.

Mahatma Gandhi

If we have no peace,
it is because we have
forgotten that we
belong to each other.

Mother Teresa

**The more you praise and
celebrate your life, the more
there is in life to celebrate.**

Oprah Winfrey

Clouds come floating into my life, no longer to carry rain or usher storm, but to add colour to my sunset sky.

Rabindranath Tagore

After silence, that which comes nearer to expressing the inexpressible is music.
Aldous Huxley

Heaven is under our feet as well as over our heads.

Henry David Thoreau

Our Quest

Finding enlightenment is a lifelong quest. It is not necessarily our sole purpose in life, but awareness of it may accompany us, and enrich our experience, as we grow and learn through the years.

Be self-aware, but do not be self-conscious. They are two different things.

The foolish man seeks happiness in the distance; the wise grows it under his feet.
J. Robert Oppenheimer

Enlightenment comes only when there is space for it. Build relaxation and leisure into your life, so that your mind, as well as your body, is free to rest.

If a man empties his purse into his head, no man can take it away from him. An investment in knowledge always pays the best interest.

Benjamin Franklin

When you meet a new person, first find out who he or she is, before telling them about yourself.

Kindness and consideration are never wasted.

He who asks a question is a fool for five minutes. He who does not ask a question remains a fool for ever.

Chinese proverb

Philosophy will clip an angel's wings.

John Keats

Enlightenment is a mystery; yet it is also as clear as day.

The best way to answer a question is to show, rather than to tell.

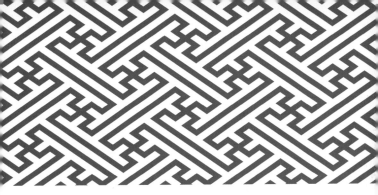

To teach how to live with uncertainty, yet without being paralysed by hesitation, is perhaps the chief thing that philosophy can do.

Bertrand Russell

We all have role models in life, whether good or bad; the trick is knowing who our role models should be, and whether they are the ones we should emulate.

No one single person can change the world; but together, day by day, we can all make small changes.

Life is what you make it.

Respect others, and you will learn to respect yourself.

Sometimes the truth hurts, and you must find the right place and time to tell it.

I long, as does every human being, to be at home wherever I find myself. *Maya Angelou*

Even in the darkest hour, we can look forward to the dawn.

The gift of enlightenment is given to few, but it is sought by many.

A mistake is simply another way of doing things.

Katharine Graham

Moments of enlightenment come to us all; it is making them last that is the difficult part.

The beauty of nature may often open our eyes to the beauty of our everyday lives.

By focussing on regrets and hopes, we deprive ourselves of joy in the here and now.

Climb the mountains and get their good tidings.
John Muir

We can only aspire to our dreams; we can't force them to come true.

Understand what you can control in life, and what you can't. You will be happier for knowing that.

Learning how to cope with failure and disappointment is as important as learning how to cope with success – and equally enlightening.

Adopt the pace of nature; her secret is patience.

Ralph Waldo Emerson

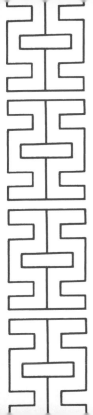

Kindness is a form of enlightenment: knowing that others feel as we do, and need to be cared for.

Life is a series of lessons that we can either ignore or learn from.

When was the last time you sat and did nothing, and just let your thoughts wander freely?

Walking, talking; caring, sharing; living, giving: that's the path to enlightenment.

A problem shared is a problem halved.

Listen before you speak; think before you answer.

I'd rather regret the things I've done than the things I haven't. *Lucille Ball*

Reliance on others is necessary in life; but make sure you allow others to be reliant on you, too.

The less you think about yourself, the more enlightened you will become.

Never let a day go by without giving thanks for it.

A man is never more truthful than when he acknowledges himself as a liar. *Mark Twain*

The river does not need to be pushed;
it flows by itself.

In times of crisis, a good friend can prove an enlightening and comforting presence.

Learn to listen; your own voice, if it's used all the time, will deafen you.

All the art of living lies in a fine mingling of letting go and holding on. *Henry Ellis*

Take pleasure in the little things of life: a hearty meal; a crackling fire; laughter of friends; the smile of a loved one.

If a job is worth doing, it's worth doing well.

Courage is a kind of salvation.

Plato

If you don't know what you're looking for in life, you will never find it.

Accept change, but make sure that your core values are unchangeable.

There is a little madness in every great soul.

Believe you can and you're halfway there.

Theodore Roosevelt

There are many ways to find enlightenment. Religious faith is only one of them.

Recognizing one's fellow human being as an equal member of humanity is one of the most basic forms of enlightenment.

Kindness, love, and consideration are not intrinsic to a child; they must be taught, along with everything else.

Faith is love taking the form of aspiration.

William Ellery Channing

Be fair to yourself, and then you will be kind to others.

Do not dwell in the past, do not dream of the future; concentrate the mind on the present moment.
Buddha

All the great religions teach the value of enlightenment in our lives.

Turn your face up to the sun; feel the wind in your hair, and the earth beneath your feet. Whatever your troubles, remember that you are alive, with all these gifts around you.

Time passes slowly for the man who allows himself to be bored.

Gratitude is the fairest blossom that springs from the soul.

Henry Ward Beecher

Learn to let go of your worry and fear. Tell yourself, they will keep till later.

Give light and people will find the way. *Ella Baker*

Ancient
Wisdom

The poets, philosophers, historians and anonymous voices of the classical world have much to tell us about enlightenment. Their thoughts, you'll find, are as relevant today as they were two thousand years ago.

Deal with the faults of others as gently as with your own.

Chinese proverb

First learn the meaning of what you say, and then speak. *Epictetus*

Do not think you will necessarily be aware of your own enlightenment.
Dōgen

Hold faithfulness and sincerity as first principles.
Confucius

As long as you're subject to birth and death, you'll never attain enlightenment.
Bodhidharma

There is in the worst of fortune the best of chance for a happy change.
Euripides

While there's life, there's hope. *Cicero*

The greatest gift is to give people your enlightenment, to share it. *Buddha*

Whatever is to make us better and happy, God has placed either openly before us or close to us. *Seneca*

I understood that the will could not be improved before the mind had been enlightened.

Johann Heinrich Lambert

When the student is ready, the master appears.

Buddha

Knowing others is wisdom, knowing yourself is enlightenment. Mastering others requires force. Mastering the self requires real strength. *Lao Tzu*

Not creating illusions is enlightenment.

Bodhidharma

To enjoy good health, to bring true happiness to one's family, to bring peace to all, one must first discipline and control one's own mind. If a man can control his mind he can find the way to Enlightenment, and all wisdom and virtue will naturally come to him. *Buddha*

There are many paths to enlightenment. Be sure to take one with a heart.
Lao Tzu

You cannot step into the same river twice. *Heraclitus*

Only one person in a million becomes enlightened without a teacher's help.

Bodhidharma

Before enlightenment – chop wood, carry water. After enlightenment – chop wood, carry water.

Zen proverb

He who has seen present things has seen all, both everything which has taken place from all eternity and everything which will be for time without end; for all things are of one kin and of one form.

Marcus Aurelius

We do not inherit the earth from our ancestors; we borrow it from our children.

The enlightened ruler is heedful,
and the good general full of caution.
Sun Tzu

**If a man will begin with certainties,
he shall end in doubts; but if he is
content to begin with doubts, he
shall end in certainties.** *Francis Bacon*

Knock on the sky and listen to the sound.
Zen proverb

An honest man is always a child.

Socrates

Where there is charity and wisdom,
there is neither fear nor ignorance.

St Francis of Assisi

First I shake the whole apple tree, that the ripest might fall. Then I climb the tree and shake each limb, and then each branch and then each twig, and then I look under each leaf.

Martin Luther

What a woman says to her lover should be written on wind and water. *Catullus*

The fish trap exists because of the fish. Once you've got the fish, you can forget the trap. The rabbit snare exists because of the rabbit. Once you've got the rabbit, you can forget the snare. Words exist because of meaning. Once you've got the meaning, you can forget the words. Where can I find a man who has forgotten words so I can talk with him? *Chuang Tzu*

Better to illuminate than merely to shine, to deliver to others contemplated truths than merely to contemplate.

Thomas Aquinas

Mix a little foolishness with your serious plans. It is lovely to be silly at the right moment.

Horace

The Obstacle is the Path.

Zen proverb

A man growing old becomes a child again.

Sophocles

There's no workman, whatsoever he be
That can work well and hastily.

Geoffrey Chaucer

It is easy to stand a pain, but difficult to stand an itch.

Chang Chao

The foot feels the foot when it feels the ground. *Buddha*

No snowflake ever falls in the wrong place.
Zen proverb

We are such stuff
As dreams are made on; and our little life
Is rounded with a sleep.
William Shakespeare

Do not seek to follow in the footsteps of the wise. Seek what they sought.

Matsuo Bashō

If the sky falls, one may hope to catch larks.

François Rabelais

Do thou restrain the haughty spirit in thy breast, for better far is gentle courtesy.

Homer

Our fears always
outnumber our dangers.

No man was ever wise by chance.

Seneca

A heart that loves is always young.

A straight oar looks bent in the water.
What matters is not merely that we see
things but how we see them.

Michel de Montaigne

And now abideth faith, hope,
charity, these three; but the
greatest of these is charity.

The Bible

Adapt yourself to the things among which your lot has been cast and love sincerely the fellow creatures with whom destiny has ordained that you shall live.

Marcus Aurelius

We are shaped by our thoughts; we become what we think. When the mind is pure, joy follows like a shadow that never leaves. **Buddha**

More than we use is more than we need.

A child may ask questions that a wise man cannot answer.

Imagination is the eye of the soul.

Joseph Joubert

To attract good fortune, spend a new coin on an old friend; share an old pleasure with a new friend; and lift up the heart of a true friend by writing his name on the wings of a dragon.

Chinese proverb

What is the first business of philosophy? To part with self-conceit. For it is impossible for anyone to begin to learn what he thinks that he already knows.

Epictetus

To high places by narrow roads.

Latin proverb

Religion is a man using a divining rod. Philosophy is a man using a pick and shovel.

Never does nature say one thing and wisdom another.

Juvenal

When one has one's hands full of truth,
it is not always wise to open them.
French proverb

Wisdom outweighs
any wealth. *Sophocles*

Truth will sooner come out of error than from confusion.

Francis Bacon

How can you prove whether at this moment we are sleeping, and all our thoughts are a dream; or whether we are awake, and talking to one another in the waking state?

Plato

By three methods we may learn wisdom: First, by reflection, which is noblest; Second, by imitation, which is easiest; and third by experience, which is the bitterest.

Confucius

Love is all we have, the only way that each can help the other.

Euripides

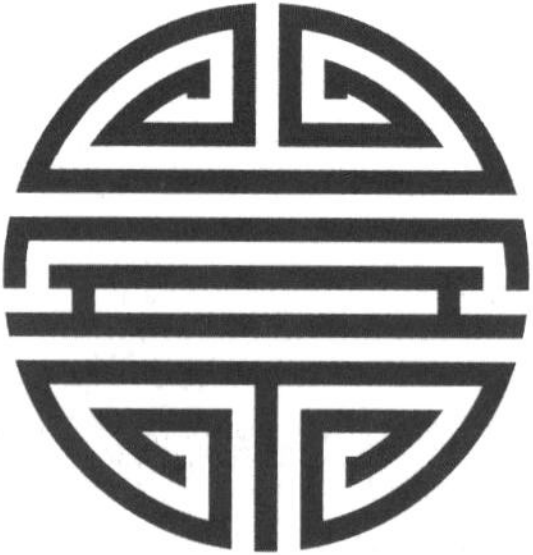

Mindfulness

Mindfulness is the new buzz word of the twenty-first century. Originally an Eastern spiritual practice involving meditation, it is now being used in Western medicine to treat a variety of health problems, both mental and physical.

Mindfulness: the state of being aware of, and attentive to what is taking place in the present.

All human beings are also dream beings. Dreaming ties all mankind together. *Jack Kerouac*

Observe first; accept next; judge last.

Time is the father of truth; its mother is our mind.

Mindfulness means not being caught up in regretting the past, or worrying about the future, but simply being aware of what is around us – what we can touch, see, hear, smell, or taste.

I keep sailing on in this middle passage. I am sailing into the wind and the dark. But I am doing my best to keep my boat steady and my sails full. *Arthur Ashe*

In situations of danger, one must take control. Our mistake is to try to control our minds when there is no danger, instead of savouring, and enjoying, the present moment.

All we can be sure of is the here and now.

Time growing old teaches all things.

Aeschylus

Mindful meditation leads to increased concentration on learning, and expanded memory, as well as self-awareness, compassion, and reflection.

Enlightenment lies in paying attention: noticing the way a tree shakes in the wind; how a bird pecks at a feeder; a cloud passing by; the sound of water running.

Our ability to savour the positive experiences in our lives is crucial to happiness, wellbeing, and enlightenment.

Technique is what you fall back on when you've run out of inspiration.

Rudolf Nureyev

Eat a hearty, nourishing meal; go for a brisk walk in the park; relax in a hot bath. They're all ways to clear your mind.

A picture is a poem without words.

Horace

Want less, and you will find you have more.

The size of the difference between what you have and what you want determines your happiness. If you want the earth, you'll never be happy.

He who has health, has hope; and he who has hope, has everything.
Thomas Carlyle

Count your blessings: health, family, work, leisure time, skills, abilities, talents, the natural world around you … the list goes on…

Love and laughter lighten the soul.

Can you imagine what I would do if I could do all I can? *Sun Tzu*

Don't be too hard on yourself. Criticizing natural emotions, like anger or jealousy, will only increase feelings of frustration. Instead, try to ask yourself, why do I feel like this?

Nobody can run fast enough to escape their own worries. They must be faced, and challenged.

If you feel there must be more to life, take a look around you. It's all right here, in front of you!

I saw the angel in the marble and carved him until I set him free.

Michelangelo

In a frantic world, find within yourself a place of stillness.

Honesty is all you need.

Cass Elliot

Meditation helps concentration, both on the small and great tasks of life.

A bird doesn't sing because it has an answer; it sings because it has a song.
Lou Holtz

Mindfulness means living with the here and now, with space, beauty, time, and whatever life brings.

Give yourself the gift of peace. Learn how to become mindful of life's blessings.

Becoming mindful is to remember the still, strong, part of yourself which cares for you, acting as a source of wisdom and support.

All water has a perfect memory and is forever trying to get back to where it was.

Toni Morrison

Listening to others will help you listen to yourself.

Lighten the burden of your over-active mind; just let your thoughts pass by, without intervening.

Today is the tomorrow we worried about yesterday.

I like nonsense, it wakes up the brain cells. Fantasy is a necessary ingredient in living, it's a way of looking at life through the wrong end of a telescope. Which is what I do, and that enables you to laugh at life's realities.

Dr Seuss

Enlightenment does not have to be an internal process. It can come by working in harmony with other like-minded people.

Beauty is a source of aspiration in human kind, and as such, reminds us of our higher being.

From time to time, throw away the plan, and the map, and instead, allow the unexpected to seduce you.

A mind that is stretched by a new experience can never go back to its old ways.

Oliver Wendell Holmes

To believe in one's dreams is to spend all of one's life asleep.
Chinese proverb

Meditation, breathing, yoga: all ways to be mindful, and to achieve enlightenment.

A man's errors are his portals of discovery.

James Joyce

Do not be overwhelmed by busy thoughts; learn to manage them, not through banishing them, but simply by letting them pass by you.

Finish each task; if you rush from one to another, you are setting your brain to high alert, as if you were being chased by a predator.

All life is an experiment.

Ralph Waldo Emerson

Mindfulness is awareness; if you walk, and it's a beautiful day, appreciate it, know that you are doing it.

Find within yourself a place of stillness, through mindful meditation. You'll find that after a while, your attention span, concentration, and memory will improve.

If you try to control the whole world, the whole world will control you.

Bring your complete attention to the experience you are having at the moment. Do not judge it, simply let it happen.

Acknowledge and accept each thought, feeling, or sensation that arises in you as you go about your daily life.

To think and to be fully alive are the same.

Hannah Arendt

Curiosity; openness; acceptance. The three elements of mindfulness.

If you look at the experience you are having as though it is completely new, and has never happened to you before, you will find yourself able to savour it to the full.

It is better to walk than curse the road.

African proverb

Mindfulness improves the immune system and alters brain function, aiding resistance to pain and recovery from negative experiences.

Intrusive thoughts, excessive brooding over events that cannot be changed, ruminating to no purpose – these are ailments of the mind that can be treated if we turn our attention to the present, the everyday, the here and now.

May our heart's garden of awakening bloom with hundreds of flowers.

Thich Nhat Hanh

We are the guardians of meaning in our lives.

Focussing on breathing, the slow intake and exhalation of breath filling our bodies, is a way of putting 'busy thoughts' to the back of our minds.

**If you think you have enough,
you are halfway to having enough.**

The moment one gives close
attention to anything, even
a blade of grass, it becomes
a mysterious, awesome,
indescribably magnificent
world in itself. *Henry Miller*

Own each moment of your experience, good, bad, or ugly.

Relief of suffering, and the dispelling of illusion, are what every human being must seek.

I believe in God, only I spell it Nature.

Frank Lloyd Wright

Recognize the importance of silence; inward attention; active listening; and being centred.

When we leave off thinking, we start living.

If we could see the miracle of a single flower clearly, our whole life would change.

Buddha

Do not live your life in the past, or in the future; live it as it happens, in the present.

Patience and diligence, like faith, remove mountains.

William Penn

Where there's life, there's hope.

Make today the start of a wonderful new adventure.

It is what you learn after you think you know it all that counts.

Our true reality is in our identity and unity with all life.

Joseph Campbell

Life is a mystery; so let the mystery be.

Kindness is an acknowledgement that another human being feels exactly as you do.

The enlightened soul often lives within the humblest, and quietest, of people.

Our achievements of today are but the sum total of our thoughts of yesterday. You are today where the thoughts of yesterday have brought you, and you will be tomorrow where the thoughts of today take you.

Blaise Pascal

Inner peace is difficult to achieve, for it is not gained by striving, but by ceasing to strive.

For yesterday is but a Dream
And Tomorrow is only a Vision;
But Today well lived makes
Every Yesterday a Dream of Happiness
And every Tomorrow a Vision of Hope.

Kālidāsa

**Knowing one does not understand is
the first step to gaining knowledge.**

Laughter is the best medicine.

I ask not for a lighter burden, but for broader shoulders.

Jewish proverb

Notice when you stop paying attention to what you are doing. Then start!

First say to yourself what you would be; then do what you have to do. *Epictetus*

Living your life on automatic pilot, multi-tasking, juggling different demands, takes its toll. If you slow down and look at the view, you may find the ride more enjoyable.

Are you 'present' or 'absent' in your day-to-day life?

All the knowledge I possess, everyone else can acquire; but my heart is my own.

Johann Wolfgang von Goethe

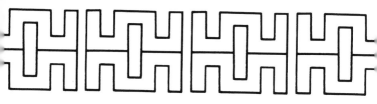

Clarity; insight; understanding. These are the hallmarks of the mindful individual.

Learn to slow down or stop the mindless chatter in your brain, that distracts attention from what is really going on around you.

When you have too much to do, step back, and prioritize. That way, you can begin to work calmly towards your goal.

However much others expect of you, do not expect too much of yourself.

Every day, find some time to sit quietly, and look at the world around you in all its beauty and variety.

And Joy is Everywhere
It is in the Earth's green covering of grass;
In the blue serenity of the Sky;
In the reckless exuberance of Spring
In the severe abstinence of grey Winter.

Rabindranath Tagore

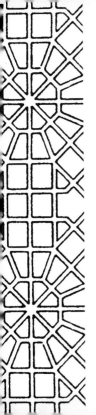

Make sure to mark your life with celebrations, holidays, and special occasions; otherwise, you will find that it flies by too quickly.

We all have to work hard in life; but spending our leisure time creatively can make all the difference to our wellbeing.

We all have our own life to pursue,
Our own kind of dream to be weaving.
And we all have some power
To make wishes come true,
As long as we keep believing.

Louisa May Alcott

Aim high, but don't let pursuing your goal become your only object in life.

I wish I could show you when you are lonely or in darkness the astonishing light of your own being.

Hafiz of Persia

Observation and concentration are the cornerstones of enlightenment.

Keep an open mind, and an open heart; that way, you will not be disappointed in your fellow human being.

To love and be loved is the purpose of your life.

It takes a deep commitment to change and an even deeper commitment to grow. *Ralph Ellison*

Make friends, not enemies, wherever and whenever you can; for if you treat others well, you'll find yourself well treated in return.

However long the night, the dawn will surely break.

The truth constantly changes, depending on your perspective.

In life, nothing is certain except the knowledge that nothing is certain.

The place to improve the world is in one's own heart and head and hands. *Robert M. Pirsig*

Beauty inspires not only the artist, but those who are touched by great art.

However far you have come, there will always be a long way to go.

You will not be punished for your anger; you will be punished by your anger. *Buddha*

Enlightenment comes with the realization that there is a greater truth than the one you already know.

Only if you despise yourself can others despise you.

There is more to life than increasing its speed. *Mahatma Gandhi*

Your treasure house is in yourself – it contains all you need.

The fragrance of the rose lingers in the mind long after it has lost its first bloom.

We cannot see our reflection in running water. It is only in still water that we can see.

Taoist proverb

**Ten thousand flowers in spring, the moon in autumn,
a cool breeze in summer, snow in winter.
If your mind isn't clouded by unnecessary things,
this is the best season of your life.** *Wu Men*

Health, contentment, and trust are your greatest possessions, freedom your greatest joy.

Buddha

Compassion is an essential part of the enlightened mind.

Listen to the rhythm of life, and if you cannot hear it, create a rhythm of your own, in time to the beat of your heart.

To touch the soul of another human being is a spiritual quest, not necessarily a religious one.

Take a rest; a field that has rested gives a bountiful crop. *Ovid*

For true enlightenment to come about, the heart and the head must act together, in unison.

It may be that the purpose of life is not to be happy, but simply to be useful; only then, if we are lucky, will happiness alight upon us, as a result of our activity.

Nobody has ever measured, not even poets, how much a heart can hold.

Zelda Fitzgerald

Always allow for the fact that you may be mistaken; only then can you be sure of being right.

A smile; a touch; a listening ear; a whispered word of comfort. Such small acts can bring a ray of light into a person's life.

The beginning is always today. *Mary Wollstonecraft*

True Understanding

Seeking true understanding may seem, to some, an impossible quest. Of course, we never reach the point where we understand everything. Yet, in order to give our lives meaning, we need to be open to the potential that learning brings through experience, whether or not we finally achieve our goal.

What is the meaning of life? To be happy and useful. *Tenzin Gyatso*

Finding your purpose in life, whatever it may be, is a well-trodden path to enlightenment.

You can create love and joy in your life; your future is in your hands, and yours alone.

Moments of fulfilment come from small, as well as great, achievements; and in these moments, we feel at peace with ourselves and the world.

Isn't it a noble, an enlightened way of spending our brief time in the sun, to work at understanding the universe and how we have come to wake up in it?

Richard Dawkins

You cannot escape suffering; you can only escape being overwhelmed by it, by facing it and challenging it every day.

Live your life in such a way that you can explore your skills and talents; for many of us, this provides a deep sense of meaning as we follow our separate paths.

Much of our joy in the universe – in the stars, the moon, the sun, in nature and the seasons – comes from sharing our delight with others.

Sometimes our fate resembles a fruit tree in winter. Who would think that those branches would turn green again and blossom, but we hope it, we know it.

Johann Wolfgang von Goethe

**Listen deeply, even to silence;
then you will begin to understand.**

You can live without thinking, or you can live constructively, attempting to reach your goals. It's your choice, and one that you cannot avoid making.

Optimism is the faith that leads to achievement. Nothing can be done without hope and confidence.
Helen Keller

Part of being human is to rise above your own particular concerns and see the entire picture.

Whatever you do, do it with love.
Then it will be well done.

If you would be a seeker after truth, it is necessary that at least once in your life you doubt, as far as possible, all things.

René Descartes

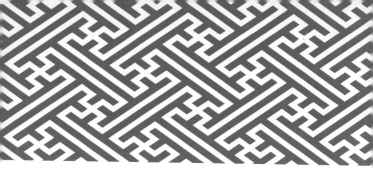

Actions speak louder than words.

Be grateful for the gift of life,
and cherish it; never make
the mistake of assuming it
is yours as a right.

All human eyes have longing in them.

Ernesto Cardenal

Nothing is certain in this world; everything is open to interpretation.

Spending time alone helps to focus the mind, and may be a route to enlightenment.

A man may fulfil the object of his existence by asking a question he cannot answer, and attempting a task he cannot achieve.

Oliver Wendell Holmes

If you are faced with a difficult task, it helps to remember those who have gone before you and achieved it.

You don't have to
have an opinion
on everything.

**A great truth is
a truth whose
opposite is
also a truth.**

Thomas Mann

Enlightenment may not come like a lightning bolt from the sky, but through a gradual realization, through work and commitment, that one has earned a rightful place in the world.

There are no nationalities, no boundaries; we are all, in essence, part of humanity.

To exist is to change, to change is to mature, to mature is to go on creating oneself endlessly.
Henri Bergson

Don't rush to achieve your goals; you may find yourself closer to where you want to be if you go more slowly.

To travel is better than to arrive.

There is nothing like a dream to create the future. *Victor Hugo*

Perseverance and patience are required if one is to seek enlightenment; courage and hope, too.

Where there's a will, there's a way.

Great things are done by a series of small things brought together.

Vincent Van Gogh

Being kind is sometimes more important than being right; and it is a less lonely business, too.

In winter, don't sit inside and wait for spring; go out into the cold and learn to appreciate the stark landscape, seeing its true structure, its bare bones, as it were.

Each night, when I go to sleep, I die. And the next morning, when I awake, I am reborn. *Mohandas Gandhi*

In the midst of confusion, hold on to the belief that you can make sense of the world, and that, one day, you will begin to understand your purpose here on earth.

There is no time like the present.

Enlightenment comes every morning, when the sun brings a new day into being. The question is, will you notice what is happening?

Birth, life, and death – each took place on the hidden side of a leaf.

Toni Morrison

There is beauty in almost everything, if only we have the eyes to see it.

The counsel you would have
another keep, keep first yourself.

**Value advice from
a person who you
know loves you, even
if you cannot follow
it; you may find that,
in the future, you will
remember it.**

Because I could not stop for Death
He kindly stopped for me
The carriage held but just ourselves
And Immortality. *Emily Dickinson*

Enduring disappointment in life, with a good grace, is a way of overcoming it, and will, at the very least, earn you your self-respect.

A healthy, happy old age is a simple aim to aspire to, but very few of us achieve it.

Youth is wasted on the young.

For everything there is a season
And a time to every purpose
under heaven. *The Bible*

Enlightenment is not the purpose of life. It comes when we look for something else that is valuable, such as knowledge; or engage in an activity that is useful, such as caring for others.

A little bird hops onto the feeder that we have set up in the garden. A small act, but a beautiful one.

In order to think clearly, one must spend time alone. Of course, not everyone wants to think clearly.

Pure love is a willingness to give without a thought of receiving anything in return. *Peace Pilgrim*

Slow help is no help.

The first step towards enlightenment is to be honest with yourself, and with others.

We come into the world and cry: that is life. We leave the world and cry: that is death.

Speak well of your friends; say nothing of your enemies.

Life is the first gift, love the second, and understanding the third.
Marge Piercy

If you allow your days to pass by without enjoying life's small pleasures, you become like a blacksmith's bellows. You breathe, but you do not live.

As you grow older, try to avoid living in the past.

Whether or not you are able to achieve your goals in life, it is important to set them, and to strive for them.

Do not listen to what people say; look at what they do.

The chance to love and be loved exists no matter where you are.

Oprah Winfrey

Finding
the Light

In most people's lives, there are fleeting moments of enlightenment, perhaps after achievements, whether in love or work, or in times of loss and sadness. How do we learn from these moments? And how can we use our knowledge to help us find contentment in our lives?

The person who has health is young; the person who owes nothing is rich.

We must love one another or die.
W. H. Auden

Conversation with a wise person can be more enlightening than years of reading books.

Choose your friends, and your pleasures in life, with care.

The moving finger writes; and, having writ,
Moves on; nor all thy Piety nor Wit
Shall lure it back to cancel half a Line
Nor all thy Tears wash out a Word of it.

Omar Khayyám

It can be just as honourable not to take revenge, as to take it.

First listen to your conscience; then to the opinion of the rest of the world.

Gratitude is the way that the heart remembers.

When the apples are ripe, they will fall; there is no need to shake the tree.

True homage comes from the heart, as well as the lips, and shows itself in deeds. *Theodore Roosevelt*

Those who say little are thought to be wise; those who say much are seen to be fools.

Don't envy others; they may have more problems than you know about, and may be struggling just as much as you are.

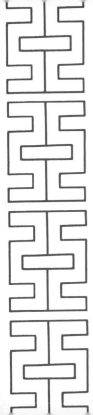

All sunshine and no rain makes a desert of the landscape.

The best protection against the vicissitudes of life is good family and friends, rather than a high wall around your house.

363

Feeling gratitude and not expressing it is like wrapping a present and not giving it.
William Arthur Ward

Take your time to make an important decision, but once you have made it, don't look back.

It is better to light a candle than to curse the darkness.

The best form of protection is to keep out of harm's way.

Ask for advice from those with a wide experience of life, not those with a wide experience of books.

Could a greater miracle take place than for us to look through each other's eyes for an instant?

Henry David Thoreau

Danger and delight often dwell together.

Don't tie a knot too tight – you may find that when the time comes to untie it, you will be unable to.

In the morning, we hope; by evening, we know.

Having anything you want, whenever you want it, dulls the flavour of life.

One should examine oneself for a very long time before thinking of condemning others. *Molière*

Those who have little may be more content than those with riches.

Do not regret growing older. It is a privilege denied to many.

To be without some of the things you want is an indispensable part of happiness.

Bertrand Russell

Don't spend too much time asking yourself how you feel. Rather, plan your day so you will eat well and get some exercise, both for mind and body.

Character is what you are; reputation is what others think you are. Be more concerned with the first.

Don't let all the things you can't do mask all the things you can.

True friendship, like true love, may take time to grow.

Work hard at work worth doing.

I start from where the world is, as it is, not from where I would like it to be. *Saul Alinsky*

What you deserve may not be what you expect.

There is always hope, always a new possibility – but sometimes it may be hiding.

Enthusiasm and energy are great gifts in a personality, and can take one a very long way in life.

Honesty is always the best policy.

Reality is merely an illusion, albeit a very persistent one.

Albert Einstein

An open mind is an enlightened mind.

There is much in life that is irrational; that is why we need reason, to understand it.

No pain, no gain; the choice is yours.

Language is a cracked kettle on which we beat out tunes for bears to dance to, while all the time we long to move the stars to pity.

Gustave Flaubert

You can't judge a book by its cover.

If you love life, make sure that you do not squander time, because that is the stuff life is made of.

All of us need solitude from time to time, to reflect on where we are, who we are, and where we are going.

Love from one being to another can only be that two solitudes come nearer, recognize and protect and comfort each other. *Han Suyin*

Events of life can make us happy or sad, but much of how we feel we carry within us all the time; we can only change that part of ourselves by our own efforts.

The artist in us is that part of us that is always alone, and needs to create an individual world, a rightful place, to live in.

When people are laughing, they're generally not killing each other.
Alan Alda

You may not find the light, but you can follow it; that way, you will at least be able to see where you are going.

Life is never easy, but ask yourself sometimes, are you making it harder than it needs to be?

All men have a sweetness in their life. That is what helps them go on. It is to that they turn when they feel too worn out.

Albert Camus

The idea that we are near to reaching our goal helps us to go on, even if we are in fact mistaken.

The real miracle is not to walk on water or thin air, but to walk on earth. Every day we are engaged in a miracle which we don't even recognize: a blue sky, white clouds, green leaves, the black, curious eyes of a child – our own two eyes. All is a miracle. *Thich Nhat Hanh*

Still waters run deep.

We sometimes look back on the hard times in our lives with great nostalgia, realizing that they were perhaps the happiest.

Two things fill the mind with ever new and increasing wonder and awe – the starry heavens above me and the moral law within me.

Immanuel Kant

What the eye doesn't see, the heart doesn't grieve.

Is it so small a thing
To have enjoy'd the sun
To have lived light in the spring
To have loved, to have thought,
to have done. *Matthew Arnold*

If you plough your own furrow in life, it may yield unexpected benefits, such as enduring respect from those around you.

There are two ways of spreading light: to be the candle or the mirror that reflects it.

Edith Wharton